To I-85 North
Exit 63

Banks House
(future development)

Office
Annex

rance

Duncan Road

Operations
Building

Original
Confederate
Fortifications

**The Battlefield
Center**

Main Loop

Intermediate Loop

**The Military
Encampment**

**The Breakthrough
Trail**

ministrative
Offices

Short Loop

Pamplin Historical Park & The National Museum of the Civil War Soldier is located in Dinwiddie County, Virginia, six miles from Petersburg and thirty miles from downtown Richmond.

PREFACE

The Civil War influenced the character and direction of America more than any single event in our nation's history. Yet the very enormity of that war has tended to obscure our vision of the men and women who shaped it, fought it, and sustained it. Pamplin Historical Park & The National Museum of the Civil War Soldier provides today's generation of Americans a unique opportunity to understand the origins, conduct, and impact of the Civil War from the perspective not of the "great men" of the 1860s, but through the eyes of ordinary citizens embroiled in an extraordinary era.

Pamplin Historical Park includes five distinct destinations, each with its own themes and facilities. The Park's three museums, pristine battlefield, and extensive costumed interpretive program explore antebellum Southern life, the impact of the Civil War on civilians, the motivation and experience of Billy Yank and Johnny Reb—the common soldier of North and South—and the conclusion of the critical Petersburg Campaign of 1864–1865.

The emphasis at Pamplin Historical Park is on interactive learning, for all ages. Whether you wish to explore the reconstructed soldier huts and camps, accept the challenge of a computerized drill sergeant to pack your knapsack, or mingle in Tudor Hall's kitchen with authentically clothed interpreters, a visit to Pamplin Historical Park will excite your senses and enrich your understanding of life in the Civil War period.

This remarkable historical campus is a gift of Robert B. Pamplin and his son, Robert B. Pamplin, Jr. Philanthropists, educators, and preservationists, the Pamplins are doing for the Civil War what the Rockefellers did for the eighteenth century at Colonial Williamsburg— but with a twist. The land now comprising the Park once belonged to the Pamplins' ancestors, the Boisseaus. Their ancestral farm has come full circle, and now you can share its powerful lessons and haunting landscapes.

This book is a wonderful introduction to the fascinating stories that unfold at Pamplin Historical Park. I invite you to enjoy it, just as I welcome you as a visitor to our Park. By "spending time" with the men and women of Civil War America, it is my hope that you will be inspired by their courage, dedication, and perseverance, and reap lessons that will enrich your own life.

A. Wilson Greene
Executive Director
Pamplin Historical Park &
The National Museum of the Civil War Soldier

PAMPLIN HISTORICAL PARK & THE NATIONAL MUSEUM OF THE
CIVIL WAR SOLDIER

PAMPLIN HISTORICAL PARK
&
THE NATIONAL MUSEUM
OF THE CIVIL WAR SOLDIER

AMERICAN ICONS   A CLOSE-UP GUIDE

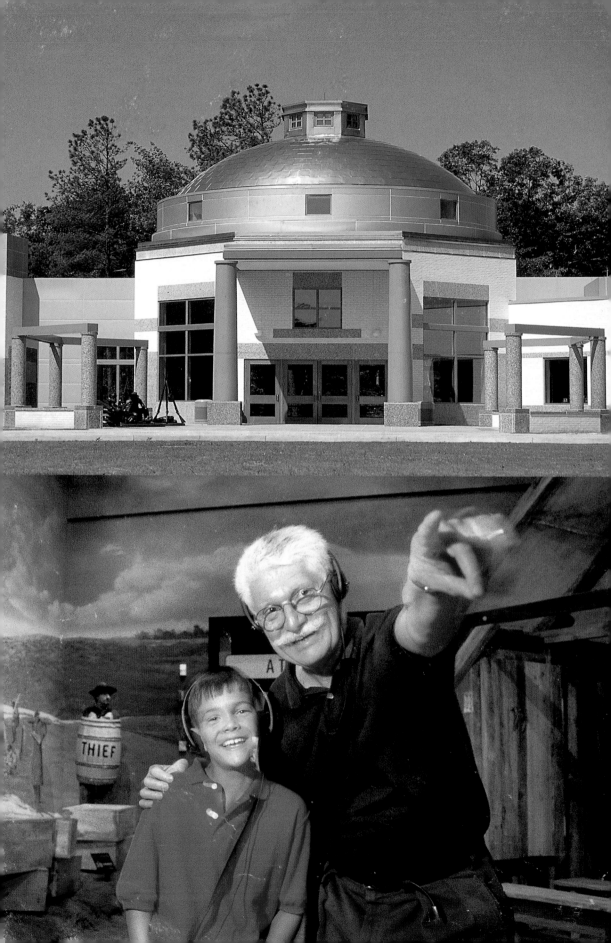

THE NATIONAL MUSEUM OF THE CIVIL WAR SOLDIER

A state-of-the-art facility dedicated to the three million men who served in the armies of the Union and Confederacy between 1861 and 1865, The National Museum of the Civil War Soldier uses the latest technology to convey what life was like for the vast majority of soldiers who attained the rank of captain or lower during America's most costly conflict.

The Museum's entrance plaza features "The Soldiers' Bivouac," an evocative bronze sculpture by Ron Tunison, the nation's preeminent contemporary sculptor of Civil War subjects. Tunison has depicted two ordinary soldiers, who could represent troops from either side. One is crouching over a small campfire, preparing a quick meal, while the other has turned his knapsack into a temporary writing desk and is penning a letter to a far-off recipient. The sculpture's theme captures the everyday heroism demonstrated by Civil War volunteers from both North and South: "My thoughts and heart are with you at home, but my duty lies here with cause and comrades."

Inside the Museum's spacious lobby, guests can visit the Civil War Store, one of the largest book and gift centers in the country dedicated exclusively to the Civil War period, or enjoy a snack at the Hardtack & Coffee Cafe. The Museum's premier attraction is a 9,000-square-foot permanent exhibit entitled "Duty Called Me Here: The Common Soldier's Experience in the American Civil War."

Above: Private Delavan S. Miller, Company H, 2nd New York Heavy Artillery Regiment, is the featured Soldier Comrade for the specially designed children's Discovery Program.

Page 1: "The Soldier's Bivouac" by Ron Tunison

Opposite, above: The entrance to the National Museum of the Civil War Soldier serves as the gateway to all of Pamplin Historical Park. Opposite, below: The Museum's interactive audio tour and lifelike exhibits appeal to visitors of all ages.

Visitors can relax over a quick meal in the Hardtack & Coffee Cafe (below) or pick up a souvenir in the Civil War Store (left).

Giles

Beidelman

Welsh

Woodcock

Berkeley

Bull

Each guest is outfitted with a compact disc player which allows the listener to choose from 45 topics keyed to exhibits throughout the museum. Visitors begin their journey by selecting one of thirteen audio "comrades" who were actual soldiers. Park staff have carefully selected men whose civilian origins and military outcomes proportionally reflect the origins and outcomes of all Civil War soldiers. At four points during the tour, visitors can hear the actual words of their comrade as he describes his motivations for joining the army, the anticipation of his first battle, his experiences in combat, and his attitudes toward remaining in the army.

Below: Realistic environments and reproduction equipment help immerse visitors in the world of the Civil War soldier.

The exhibit itself consists of seven galleries in which guests may explore the soldiers' experiences. Exhibits include interactive computer games and re-creations of summer and winter camps, a field hospital amputation (on video), a fire-and-brimstone camp sermon, and a march into battle in the museum's most unusual gallery, "Trial By Fire." Murals by renowned military artist Keith Rocco complement period photographs and more than 1,000 artifacts to immerse visitors in the Civil War soldier's world.

The museum's introductory gallery sets the stage for the Civil War. When hostilities erupted in 1861, most Americans lived on farms or in small towns. Their lives centered around family, religion, and community. As

citizens, their first loyalty was to their state—and particularly the local region they called home. Americans in 1861 followed politics closely—especially the debate over the expansion of slavery into the new Western territories. Most white Southerners did not own slaves, but virtually all of them accepted slavery as the best possible system of labor or as the only way the races could coexist successfully. White Northerners shared similar racial biases, although a growing number believed slavery was immoral. The North opposed expanding slavery mostly for economic reasons: as unfair competition with farms and businesses that used free labor. When Abraham Lincoln was elected president on a platform opposing new slave states, the conflict reached a crisis.

"A Soldier's Life" immerses visitors in an early-war military camp. Across the country, citizens on both sides rushed to defend their liberty. Most recruits marched into camp with volunteer and militia companies, proudly sponsored by their home communities. Their regiment became their new home.

The experiences of Civil War soldiers were strikingly similar, whether they came from the North or the South. Men on both sides learned the same drills and faced many of the same dangers. Most soldiers entering the war believed passionately in their cause—whether Union or Confederate—and hoped they would have a chance to fight to uphold what they perceived as the true legacy of the American Revolution.

"On the March" focuses on army organization and the logistics of moving troops from camp into battle. Thousands of men, animals, supply wagons, and artillery pieces trundled over narrow country roads; as they passed, the impact of so many feet, hooves, and wheels transformed the landscape. Most soldiers were unprepared for their first march and grew confused and

Above: This artwork by Keith Rocco, entitled "Ready for the March," is one of seven huge murals which add depth to the galleries.

Opposite, top: Choose a Comrade from a group of twelve real soldiers in "Duty Called Me Here." Photographs of those men appear above from left to right: Private Valerius Cincinnatus Giles, Company B, 4th Texas Infantry Regiment; Private George Washington Beidelman, Company C, 71st Pennsylvania Infantry Regiment; Sergeant Peter Welsh, Company K, 28th Massachusetts Infantry Regiment; Lieutenant William Marcus Woodcock, Company B, 9th Kentucky (U. S.) Infantry Regiment; Private Henry Robinson Berkeley, Amherst (Virginia) Battery; Sergeant William Jeffery Bull, Lesueur's (Missouri) Battery (The other comrades are shown on page 9.)

Below: Music was an integral part of life in Civil War armies.

1

Militia uniforms were often very fashionable. This is the uniform of the Governor's Horse Guards of New Hampshire.

2

Color did not always indicate side. This gray jacket was worn by Private Milton Wolfe of the 28th Pennsylvania Infantry.

3

Early in the war, many soldiers believed armored vests would save their lives.

4

The frock coat was the official uniform of the U. S. infantry. This one was worn by Sergeant Charles Liscom of the 26th Iowa Regiment.

5

This Confederate enlisted man's jacket was worn by Captain Edward Marsh of the 4th North Carolina Infantry.

angry at the constant stopping and starting. Inwardly, each wondered whether he would stand his ground or be killed in the coming battle—and whether he could kill, if called upon to do so. As the war progressed, the men hardened, and before long most could easily march twelve miles a day, and up to thirty if necessary.

"Trial By Fire" gives visitors a taste of actual Civil War combat. Although combat accounted for only a tiny fraction of a soldier's time, it was surely the most memorable and dramatic aspect of military life in the Civil War.

The combination of modern weapons and outdated tactics made the Civil War the bloodiest conflict in American history. Infantrymen marched into battle in tight formation carrying a new weapon—the "rifle-musket." This modern firearm had a spiral-grooved inner barrel, or "bore," which spun the bullet, stabilizing it and giving it five times the accuracy of a smoothbore musket-ball. These new weapons could be fired up

to three times a minute, and enemy soldiers fell in waves, struck down by repeated, deadly volleys as they marched shoulder-to-shoulder. Survivors usually dispersed and were forced to retreat before they reached their goal.

Civil War soldiers fought in more than 10,000 engagements during the four years of war. Ultimately, more than 200,000 soldiers lost their lives in combat.

Besides emerging untouched, "A Soldier's Fate" describes the three possible outcomes that awaited a Civil War soldier on the battlefield. During the course of the war, a soldier ran about a one-in-fifteen risk of being killed or mortally wounded in battle; about one in eight were wounded but survived.

Both Union and Confederate prisoners suffered intensely from disease and malnutrition. Roughly one in thirteen soldiers were captured by the enemy, and about one in seven prisoners died while in captivity.

This nonregulation jacket was worn by First Sergeant Charles Hunter of the 88th Pennsylvania Infantry.

Captain Chesley Herbert of the 3rd South Carolina Infantry wore a typical officer's frock coat.

Many Civil War uniforms were edged in colored braid to indicate the soldier's branch of service: blue for infantry, yellow for cavalry, and red for artillery.

Musicians' uniforms were decorated so they could be easily recognized by officers.

Bugler Henry Lewis of the 1st Rhode Island Light Artillery had this jacket specially made.

"Surviving in the Field" places visitors in the middle of a late-war winter camp. Armies usually suspended their campaigns in late autumn as rain, snow, freezing, and thawing turned dirt roads into impassable quagmires. Commanders established camp and waited for spring to dry the mud. A few winter camps provided barracks or other permanent shelters, but most soldiers were left to their own resources. Messmates and friends often banded together to build huts and lodges. They furnished their temporary homes with crates and boxes, and hung newspaper like wallpaper at home—a place they had not seen in many months and might never see again.

Above: Amputation was the most common surgical operation during the Civil War. This sophisticated procedure greatly increased a wounded soldier's chance of survival.

Opposite, top: Civil War weapons varied widely in style and effectiveness. Some appeared fearsome but were useless.

Right: A common punishment for disobedience in the army was to wear a "barrel shirt" for several hours.

Below: Crude grave markers were occasionally erected for fallen comrades, but the identity of most soldiers buried in Civil War graves is unknown.

Most found winter camp a relief—staying in one place and sleeping in a warm, dry shelter. At first, soldiers mended their clothes, trimmed their beards, took a long-overdue bath, and settled into a quiet lifestyle with familiar duties. But before long many began to grow impatient with the dull routine. Unable to return home, and with little to do but wait, they turned their thoughts to the trials already faced and steeled themselves for the battles that lay ahead as the war continued with no end in sight.

"A Test of Faith," the subject of the museum's final gallery, examines the moral issues each soldier faced as the war dragged on. Where did his duty lie? Was his cause still worth fighting for? Some veterans came to feel they had served their country long enough and that their duty was now to take care of their families at home. Many resented serving beside new recruits, draftees, and paid substitutes, or "bounty men." Moreover, the Emancipation Proclamation and the Union army's subsequent recruitment of black soldiers brought deep divisions on both sides.

Despite hardships, dangers, and faltering convictions, most soldiers chose to remain in active service. Some survived to finish the war as victors; while the rest left the field in defeat after sacrificing all they had.

Civil War soldiers on both sides were driven by a belief in their cause and a sense of duty to their country and community. That commitment enabled them to endure the hardships of a soldier's life and shape the history of this nation. Their willingness to sacrifice their own lives transformed the lives of countless others. It is that willingness to sacrifice—the extraordinary efforts of ordinary American citizens in extreme circumstances—that we honor.

Below: Life in winter camp was tedious. Most soldiers tried to keep in contact with their family through letters.

Inset: Six of the twelve comrades featured in "Duty Called Me Here." From left to right: Corporal Elisha Stockwell, Jr., Company I, 14th Wisconsin Infantry Regiment; Private Charles Brandegee, Private, Company I, 5th New York Infantry Regiment; Lieutenant George Job Huntley, Company I, 34th North Carolina Infantry Regiment; Private Eli Pinson Landers, Company H, 16th Georgia Infantry Regiment;Sergeant Alexander Herritage Newton, Company E, 29th Connecticut Infantry Regiment; Private William C. H. Reeder, Company A, 20th Indiana Infantry Regiment.

Stockwell   **Brandegee**   **Huntley**   **Landers**   **Newton**   **Reeder**

Tudor Hall

Tudor Hall does not fit the stereotypical image of an antebellum (pre–Civil War) Southern plantation. The building's Greek revival architecture is subtle, the porches can accommodate only a few sippers of mint juleps, and the home's modest size suggests owners of middling rather than extravagant means.

The family that built and lived at Tudor Hall between 1812 and 1864 resided firmly in the upper crust of Virginia society. That family, the Boisseaus (pronounced BOY-saw), lived a step below the first families of Virginia whose mansions along the James River or on plateaus in the Piedmont bespoke many generations of inherited wealth. Nevertheless, the owners of Tudor Hall occupied the next rung on Virginia's socio-economic ladder. Their substantial wealth was largely due to an agricultural productivity which depended on slave labor.

Tudor Hall's story begins in 1810 when William E. Boisseau acquired 100 acres near the headwaters of Arthur's Swamp. A descendant of French Huguenots who settled in Dinwiddie County during the 1730s, William began building a home there in about 1812. A substantial dwelling designed in the popular

Pages 10–11: Rear view of Tudor Hall shows entrances to "A Land Worth Fighting For" exhibit and restored interior rooms.

Opposite: Tudor Hall's west parlor may have served as a dining room and family sitting room for the Boisseaus.

Below: Tudor Hall incorporated several architectural styles—Georgian, Federal, and Greek Revival.

Federal style on a raised brick basement, Tudor Hall quickly became the seat of a large agricultural operation. Tobacco was the cash crop in southside Virginia at that time, and William Boisseau grew the popular weed on an ever-expanding land base that eventually reached nearly 1,000 acres. Boisseau raised seven children at Tudor Hall and employed as many as 50 slaves on his plantation.

Upon William's death, Tudor Hall became the responsibility of his son, Joseph G. Boisseau, and his wife, Ann. The plantation changed dramatically during the younger Boisseaus' tenancy. In the 1850s, Joseph expanded the home to accommodate a growing family and to reflect current architectural tastes. He built a one-bay extension on the east side of the house, creating two new rooms and a center hall and stairway. He also renovated the interior woodwork, staircase, and building exterior in the Greek revival style, although much less extravagantly than what could be seen at the huge cotton mansions popular in the lower South at the time.

What went on outside the house also changed during Joseph's occupancy. Years of tobacco cultivation had depleted the plantation's soil, and profits declined with lower yields. Many large farms in Virginia began turning to grain crops as an alternative to tobacco, and by the 1850s, Tudor Hall was growing wheat, corn, and oats. These crops were less labor-intensive, allowing Joseph to reduce the number of slaves at Tudor Hall to eighteen by 1860. The farm had dwindled to less than 250 acres, but Tudor Hall retained a privileged place in Dinwiddie County's social and

Above: Joseph and Ann Boisseau's bed chamber includes furnishings typical of the 1850s and 1860s. The glazed chintz bed coverings, printed with a fashionable Oriole pattern adapted from John James Audubon's paintings, were imported from France.

The room at near right represents the private quarters of Lieutenant James Fitz James Caldwell. While at Tudor Hall, he wrote most of a manuscript on the history of McGowan's South Carolina brigade. At far right, a room representing the sleeping quarters of a number of McGowan's staff officers.

economic hierarchy. The Boisseaus continued to thrive until the clouds of war descended on the South in 1861 and threatened to undermine the foundations of Virginia's agricultural prosperity.

Joseph was too old to serve in the Confederate army, but the Civil War affected everything about daily living at Tudor Hall. The most dramatic impact of all came with the arrival of Brigadier General Samuel McGowan during the autumn of 1864. McGowan commanded a brigade of South Carolinians in General Robert E. Lee's Army of Northern Virginia and needed a place for himself and his 1,400 men to live during the fall and winter. The general took over Tudor Hall for his headquarters, and his troops established camps throughout the woods and fields of the Boisseau plantation. Joseph and Ann left their home and found shelter elsewhere, probably with friends and relatives in Petersburg as the friendly soldiers systematically commandeered the fences, woodlots, and whatever livestock the Boisseaus left behind.

Below: Tudor Hall's east parlor may have served as McGowan's brigade headquarters. The general and his staff would have used a mix of military and civilian furniture. Trunks and field desks would have held various forms, documents, and ledgers. In quieter moments, the officers might have played table games to pass the time.

Right: Original artifacts, modern graphics and reproductions are highlights of "A Land Worth Fighting For."

Opposite: Each of McGowan's staff officers claimed his own area in the headquarters room where he toiled at the endless paperwork that characterizes armies.

Below: Audio units provide information on Tudor Hall's furnished rooms.

General McGowan left Tudor Hall on March 29, 1865, to meet a military emergency elsewhere along the Petersburg fortifications. Four days later, a massive Union attack swept across the Boisseau plantation. Hundreds of Confederate soldiers were taken prisoner; General Lee was forced to abandon Petersburg and Richmond that night. The Civil War in Virginia would last just one more week.

Like many other white Southerners in the aftermath of the Civil War, Joseph and Ann Boisseau faced economic ruin. Not only was their farm left in a shambles after six months of military occupation, but they were no longer slaveowners. In 1869,

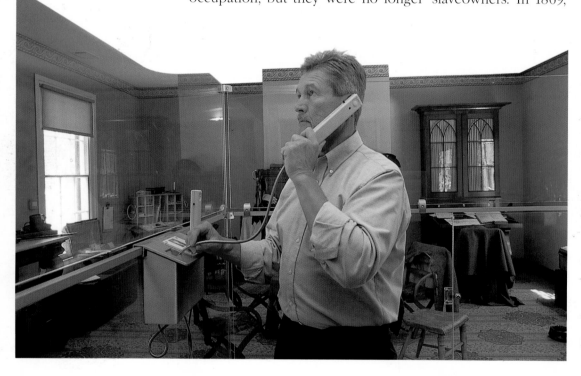

following a pattern repeated often throughout the devastated South, Joseph sold Tudor Hall to a Northerner, Asahel Gerow of New York State. The Gerows turned the property back into a productive farm, and Tudor Hall stayed in the Gerow family for several generations, during which time northern Dinwiddie County was transformed from plantation country into a region of small farms and Petersburg suburbs.

The last descendant of the Gerows to reside at Tudor Hall passed away in 1994. By then, Robert Pamplin and his son, direct descendants of the Boisseaus, had acquired a portion of the Tudor Hall estate with the intention of establishing a historical park on the site. Their acquisition of Tudor Hall brought the property back into the hands of the family that originally built the plantation nearly two centuries earlier.

Today, Tudor Hall has been fully restored to its appearance prior to the outbreak of the Civil War. Five furnished rooms reflect both the Boisseaus' occupancy in the spring of 1864 and General McGowan's tenancy during the following winter. The furnishings are all period pieces carefully selected to resemble the style of the original home. Tudor Hall's English basement houses a multi-media exhibit entitled "A Land Worth Fighting For," which addresses the Tudor Hall story in the context of Southern history. Interactive computer exhibits, large dioramas, and a number of historical photographs and artifacts help explain Tudor Hall's unique historical significance.

The plantation's grounds are also undergoing restoration. Several outbuildings are springing up around the main house to reflect the busy agricultural enterprise that was at the heart of Tudor Hall's prosperity. A kitchen and attached servants' quarters introduce the story of the black Americans' contribution to Tudor Hall's past. Visitors may interact with costumed interpreters who bring to life the rich story of this representative Virginia plantation.

Tudor Hall is not noted for architectural splendor and or distinguished owners but stands as a living example of Southern plantation life in the Civil War era—a family estate caught up in the swirl of history.

Opposite: Costumed interpreters bring the civilian and military history of Tudor Hall to life.

Overleaf: The unique design of Pamplin Historical Park's Battlefield Center beckons visitors to relive The Breakthrough.

Along the Breakthrough Trail, visitors can see Confederate earthworks constructed during the winter of 1864–1865.

THE BREAKTHROUGH

In the summer of 1864, Union armies led by Lieutenant General Ulysses S. Grant closed in on the Confederate capital at Richmond. Having failed to defeat General Robert E. Lee's Army of Northern Virginia in open battle, Grant decided to capture Petersburg. Many of the roads and railroads that brought badly needed supplies into Richmond passed through Petersburg. If the Federals could take that city, Lee would be forced to abandon the capital. The initial Union attack in June failed, and Grant was forced to conduct siege operations. Over the next several months, his men gradually stretched their entrenchments to the west, disrupting several supply routes.

Robert E. Lee

Following the Battle of Globe Tavern in late August 1864, Grant's army permanently cut the Petersburg and Weldon Railroad at that spot. Lee's army could still draw supplies from that railroad, however. Trains traveling from North Carolina could reach Stony Creek Station eighteen miles below Petersburg. From that point, supplies were transferred to wagons and carted to Dinwiddie Court House and thence to Petersburg via the Boydton Plank Road. Lee's engineers began extending the army's trench lines westward from Petersburg in September 1864 to protect the Plank Road. This expansion included the earthworks now preserved in Pamplin Historical Park.

Union troops failed to reach and cut the Boydton road in late September during the Battle of Peebles' Farm. Throughout the following months, Confederate troops established camps in the area and worked to strengthen the line of fortifications, which ultimately stretched to Hatcher's Run. Brigadier General Samuel McGowan's South Carolina brigade built entrenchments across the Boisseau farm, where they were stationed. McGowan soon moved into Tudor Hall, making it his brigade's headquarters. The South Carolinians remained in their winter camps, performing picket duty and strengthening their earthworks until the spring campaign began. Grant sent portions of his army toward Lee's right flank with the mission of capturing the South Side Railroad, and Lee responded by shifting some of his brigades to meet this threat. Late in the day on March 29, 1865, most of McGowan's

Ulysses S. Grant

brigade left the fortifications near Tudor Hall and moved to new positions south of Hatcher's Run. Brigadier General James H. Lane's North Carolina brigade replaced the South Carolinians at the Boisseau farm.

On April 1, Union forces attacked and defeated the Confederates in the Battle of Five Forks, and this victory opened the way toward the South Side Railroad. Grant sensed that the initiative was clearly in his favor. He ordered Major General George G. Meade to make "a general assault along the lines" on the morning of April 2. Meade directed these orders to Major General Horatio G. Wright, whose Sixth Corps troops were poised directly in front of the trenches held by Lane's brigade, and instructed him to attack at four o'clock in the morning.

Wright's plan called for his men to assail the Confederate defenses as silently as possible. Division commanders formed their units near the Union picket line, from which they would advance at the discharge of a single cannon. The attack formation resembled a wedge—one division in the center with a division slightly behind it on the left and right. Once the Union troops had cut the

James H. Lane

Samuel McGowan

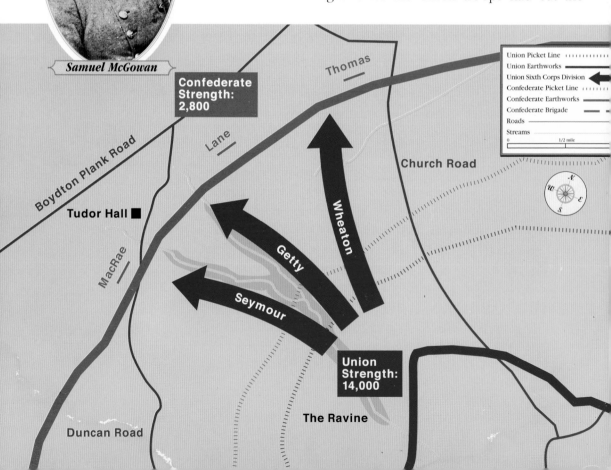

Confederate Strength: 2,800

Thomas

Union Picket Line
Union Earthworks
Union Sixth Corps Division
Confederate Picket Line
Confederate Earthworks
Confederate Brigade
Roads
Streams
0   1/2 mile

Boydton Plank Road

Lane

Church Road

Tudor Hall ■

MacRae

Wheaton

Getty

Seymour

Union Strength: 14,000

The Ravine

Duncan Road

Confederate line, they would seize the Boydton Plank Road and concentrate on capturing the South Side Railroad. Shortly after midnight, Wright's assault formation began to take shape. Brigadier General Lewis Grant's Vermont brigade was the leading unit in the assault. His men would guide their advance along a ravine that ran directly toward and through the Confederate entrenchments.

Wright postponed the assault until 4:40 a.m., when the first glimmer of morning light faintly illuminated the eastern sky. His 14,000 men, with fixed bayonets and uncapped muskets, moved forward across the open ground to their front. Orders had been given to both commanders and soldiers to advance without firing and to force their way through any *abatis* (obstructions) into the Confederate works. Small groups of pioneers carrying axes preceded the infantrymen to hack passages through these obstacles, the Civil War version of barbed wire.

Major General Horatio G. Wright sat for this photograph outside his tent in 1864. His headquarters flag now hangs in the Battlefield Center.

As the Federals moved forward, the Vermonters rose to their feet and took up the advance. Just as they reached the Confederate picket line, a scattered volley shattered the silence. Confederate artillery roared on their left and right, causing the Vermonters to waver. Fortunately for the Federals, most of the Confederate artillery fire passed overhead. Guiding on the ravine, Grant's men soon neared the main line of earthworks. Working their way through a double line of *abatis*, the Federals rushed toward the Confederate works and let loose "one full, deep, mighty cheer." All formations had been broken after coming through the *abatis*, and the four regiments of Lane's brigade laid down a heavy fire upon the attackers. However, the Confederates could not hold them back. Within minutes, the Federals were on top of the parapets and entering the works.

Shortly after 5 a.m., the troops of the Sixth Corps breached the Confederate defenses on the Boisseau farm, capturing some of the defenders and routing the rest in disorder to the northeast.

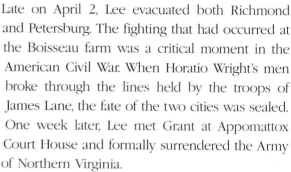

Charles G. Gould

Above: Charles G. Gould of the 5th Vermont Infantry won the Medal of Honor for his actions during The Breakthrough.

Below: A reproduction cannon stands as a silent sentinel in an artillery redan constructed by McGowan's South Carolinians.

Most of Wright's troops turned to the left after piercing Lane's line and moved along the works toward Hatcher's Run. This effort overran the entire Confederate line, and the remnants of the grayclad defenders streamed toward the Appomattox River and safety. Regrouping, the troops of the Sixth Corps turned and moved back toward Petersburg. Men of three other corps joined them as they closed in on the city's western defenses. It appeared that the fall of Petersburg was only a matter of time. Fortunately for Lee and his army, the small garrison in Fort Gregg held out long enough to allow troops from Richmond to file into the works from Battery 45 to the Appomattox River. Knowing the next day would bring him a victory, Grant refused to order an attack on this inner line. The fighting came to an end around dark.

Late on April 2, Lee evacuated both Richmond and Petersburg. The fighting that had occurred at the Boisseau farm was a critical moment in the American Civil War. When Horatio Wright's men broke through the lines held by the troops of James Lane, the fate of the two cities was sealed. One week later, Lee met Grant at Appomattox Court House and formally surrendered the Army of Northern Virginia.

Above: Union troops overrun Confederate fortifications at Petersburg.

A visit to the historic battlefield of April 2, 1865, begins at the park's Battlefield Center. The award-winning design of the Center mimics the shape of the Confederate fortifications. Inside, exhibits provide orientation to the park's earthworks and the pivotal Breakthrough of General Robert E. Lee's Petersburg defenses. Guests may view an audio-visual presentation, a fiber-optics map, and displays of authentic artifacts such as flags, weapons, and uniforms relating to events at this site. Visitors will also find refreshments, a rest area, and bathroom facilities.

Left: Headquarters flag of Major General Horatio G. Wright's Sixth Army Corps.

Just outside the Battlefield Center, Pamplin Historical Park's Breakthrough Trail leads visitors into the heart of the battlefield. A system of gentle pathways features three separate loops ranging in distance from half a mile to nearly two miles, passing through some of the finest Civil War earthwork fortifications in the United States. Walkers will also discover artillery positions, a traverse, two rarely seen military dams, Confederate picket posts or rifle pits, the site of a prewar house, and reconstructed soldier huts. Most of the terrain along the trail is level, and the pathway itself is maintained for smooth walking. A series of interpretive signs, some with recorded messages, describes the dramatic events that occurred here on the Boisseau farm in the spring of 1865.

Below: Confederate picket posts resemble foxholes from World War II and served as an early warning system for the main line of earthworks.

THE PAMPLIN PARK VISION

Above: Robert B. Pamplin, Jr. (standing) and Robert B. Pamplin now reside in Portland, Oregon.

Preceding pages: A sampling of the many life-sized dioramas in The National Museum of the Civil War Soldier. This gallery, entitled "A Soldier's Life," features murals by Keith Rocco depicting (inset, left to right): a blacksmith at a quartermaster depot; a group of soldiers waiting to be fed during a company "Mess Call"; women, possibly officers' wives or religious workers, arriving at a winter camp; and mounted officers reviewing a training drill.

Pamplin Historical Park & The National Museum of the Civil War Soldier reflects the vision and philosophy of Robert Boisseau Pamplin, Jr., and his father, Robert B. Pamplin. These two remarkable men have created a historic site to educate visitors from around the world about the American Civil War, the men who fought it, and the entire generation who endured it.

Pamplin Historical Park occupies land which once belonged to William Boisseau, a direct ancestor of the Pamplins. After the Civil War, Boisseau's son was forced to sell his holdings, but the family remained in the area. Robert B. Pamplin was born some fifty years after the Civil War on a modest farm about three miles from Pamplin Historical Park. He attended local schools and graduated with a degree in business from Virginia Tech.

Robert Pamplin began his career with Georgia Hardwood Lumber as the company's fifth employee. Georgia Hardwood Lumber grew into Georgia-Pacific Corporation, and Robert Pamplin served as its Chairman and Chief Executive Officer for many years. Since his retirement in 1976, Robert Pamplin has headed the R. B. Pamplin Corporation, which is involved in a variety of manufacturing enterprises and is one of the largest privately-held companies in the Northwest. The Pamplin family has maintained a long tradition of education-oriented philanthropy including support for a number of colleges and universities and providing scholarships for deserving students. In 1992, Bob Pamplin and his father seized an opportunity to create an educational "campus" of their own in Dinwiddie County. Inspired by their abiding interest in history, particularly that of the Civil War, and a reverence for their own family, the Pamplins set out to preserve the historic Civil War battlefield and restore Tudor Hall, the former Boisseau family home, as an unparalleled learning center documenting the history of the antebellum South as well as the men who fought on both sides of the Civil War. This privately-owned educational complex offers visitors from all walks of life a unique opportunity to learn about a pivotal chapter of our nation's history.

Construction of Pamplin Historical Park & The National Museum of the Civil War Soldier was made possible by contributions of over

$23 million by the Pamplin Foundation. Plans are underway for significant expansion culminating in the Civil War sesquicentennial anniversary in 2011.

Correspondence to the Pamplins may be directed to the Pamplin Foundation, 6125 Boydton Plank Road, Petersburg, VA 23803.

SUGGESTED READING

Benson, Susan Williams, ed. *Berry Benson's Civil War Book*. Athens: University of Georgia Press, 1962 (reprint, 1992).

Bergeron, Arthur W., Jr. *Tudor Hall: The Boisseau Family Farm*. Richmond, Va.: The Dietz Press, 1998.

Billings, John D. *Hard Tack and Coffee: The Unwritten Story of Army Life*. Williamstown: Corner House Publishers, 1993.

Calkins, Chris M. *The Appomattox Campaign, March 29–April 9, 1865*. Conshohocken, Pa.: Combined Books, 1997.

Daniel, Larry J. *Soldiering in the Army of Tennessee: A Portrait of Life in the Confederate Army*. Chapel Hill: University of North Carolina Press, 1991.

Davis, William C. *Death in the Trenches: Grant at Petersburg*. Alexandria, Va.: Time-Life Books, 1986.

Genovese, Eugene D. *Roll, Jordan, Roll: The World the Slaves Made*. New York: Pantheon Books, 1974.

Greene, A. Wilson. *Breaking the Backbone of the Rebellion: The Final Battles of the Petersburg Campaign*. Mason City, Iowa: Savas Publishing Co., 2000.

Hess, Earl J. *The Union Soldier in Battle: Enduring the Ordeal of Combat*. Lawrence: University Press of Kansas, 1997.

Humphreys, Andrew A. *The Virginia Campaign of '64 and '65*. New York: Charles Scribner's Sons, 1883; reprinted ed., Wilmington, N. C.: Broadfoot Publishing Co., 1989.

Jones, Richard L. *Dinwiddie County: Carrefour of the Commonwealth*. Richmond, Va.: Whittet & Shepperson, 1976.

Korn, Jerry. *Pursuit to Appomattox: The Last Battles*. Alexandria, Va.: Time-Life Books, 1987.

Linderman, Gerald F. *Embattled Courage: The Experience of Combat in the American Civil War.* New York: The Free Press, 1987.

McCarthy, Carlton. *Detailed Minutiae of Soldier Life in the Army of Northern Virginia, 1861–1865.* Richmond, Va.: Carlton McCarthy and Company, 1882; reprint edition, Lincoln: University of Nebraska Press, 1993.

McPherson, James M. *For Cause and Comrades: Why Men Fought in the Civil War.* New York: Oxford University Press, 1997.

Mitchell, Reid. *Civil War Soldiers: Their Expectations and Their Experiences.* New York: Viking Penguin, 1988.

Power, J. Tracy. *Lee's Miserables: Life in the Army of Northern Virginia from the Wilderness to Appomattox.* Chapel Hill: University of North Carolina Press, 1999.

Robertson, James I., Jr. *General A. P. Hill: The Story of a Confederate Warrior.* New York: Random House, 1987.

Robertson, James I., Jr. *Soldiers Blue and Gray.* Columbia: University of South Carolina Press, 1988.

Trudeau, Noah Andre. *The Last Citadel: Petersburg, Virginia, June 1864–April 1865.* Boston: Little, Brown, 1991.

Vlach, John Michael. *Back of the Big House: The Architecture of Plantation Slavery.* Chapel Hill: University of North Carolina Press, 1993.

Wiley, Bell I. *The Life of Billy Yank: The Common Soldier of the Union.* Reprint, Baton Rouge: Louisiana State University Press, 1978.

Wiley, Bell I. *The Life of Johnny Reb: The Common Soldier of the Confederacy.* Reprint, Baton Rouge: Louisiana State University Press, 1978.

Equipping and feeding the huge numbers of men in Civil War armies required vast quantities of material and thousands of mules and horses to pull the supply wagons.

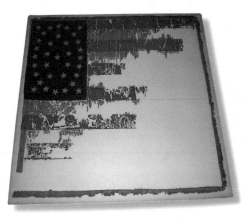

Remains of a United States national flag, perhaps carried by an artillery unit.

Flag of the 27th South Carolina Infantry Regiment.

United States regulation pattern cavalry flag.

ESTIMATED NUMBERS AND LOSSES

State	Served	Died
Alabama	82,545	1,811
Arkansas	63,815	8,575
California	15,725	573
Connecticut	55,864	5,354
Delaware	12,284	882
District of Columbia	16,534	290
Florida	17,334	2,561
Georgia	123,486	10,989
Illinois	259,092	34,834
Indiana	196,363	26,672
Iowa	76,242	13,001
Kansas	20,149	2,630
Kentucky	115,760	10,774
Louisiana	85,096	7,490
Maine	70,107	9,398
Maryland	76,638	2,982
Massachusetts	146,730	13,942
Michigan	87,364	14,753
Minnesota	24,020	2,584
Mississippi	96,414	22,833
Missouri	139,111	13,885
Nevada	1,080	33
New Hampshire	33,937	4,882
New Jersey	76,814	5,754
New York	448,850	46,534
North Carolina	128,191	40,635
Ohio	313,180	35,475
Oregon	1,810	45
Pennsylvania	337,936	33,183
Rhode Island	23,236	1,321
South Carolina	80,462	17,682
Tennessee	267,717	13,191
Texas	92,012	3,990
Vermont	33,288	5,224
Virginia	175,723	14,836
West Virginia	32,068	4,017
Wisconsin	91,327	12,301